How Fruits and Vegetables Grow

Carrots
Grow Underground

by Mari Schuh

Consulting Editor: Gail Saunders-Smith, PhD

Consultant: Sarah Pounders, education specialist
National Gardening Association

CAPSTONE PRESS
a capstone imprint

Pebble Books are published by Capstone Press,
1710 Roe Crest Drive, North Mankato, Minnesota 56003.
www.capstonepub.com

Library of Congress Cataloging-in-Publication Data
Schuh, Mari C., 1975–
    Carrots grow underground / by Mari Schuh.
        p. cm.—(Pebble books. How fruits and vegetables grow)
    Summary: "Simple text and photographs describe how carrots grow
underground"—Provided by publisher.
    Includes bibliographical references and index.
    ISBN 978-1-4296-5280-3 (library binding)
    ISBN 978-1-4296-6185-0 (paperback)
    1. Carrots—Juvenile literature. I. Title. II. Series: Pebble (Mankato, Minn.). How
fruits and vegetables grow.
    SB351.C3S38 2011
    635'.13—dc22
                                                                    2010025471

Note to Parents and Teachers

The How Fruits and Vegetables Grow set supports national science
standards related to life science. This book describes and illustrates
how carrots grow. The images support early readers in understanding
the text. The repetition of words and phrases helps early readers learn
new words. This book also introduces early readers to subject-specific
vocabulary words, which are defined in the Glossary section. Early
readers may need assistance to read some words and to use the Table
of Contents, Glossary, Read More, Internet Sites, and Index sections of
the book.

Printed in the United States   5685

Table of Contents

Under the Soil

Green stems and leaves sprout from the soil. Underground, vegetables grow larger and larger every day.

Life Cycle of a Carrot

seeds

seedling

carrots

flowers

Plant roots grow underground. People eat the roots of some plants. Carrots are one kind of root vegetable.

Growing

Carrots start as tiny seeds.
They are planted in
cool weather. In one to
three weeks, seedlings slowly
grow above the soil.

10

Under the soil, the carrots grow longer and thicker. Deep, loose soil helps carrots grow long and straight.

Long stems and lacy leaves grow from the carrot tops.

After two to three months,
crunchy vegetables
are pulled from the ground.

Flowers and Seeds

Carrots that stay underground all winter grow flowers and seeds the next year. Later, the tiny carrot seeds become new carrot plants.

radishes

beets

parsnips

Many Vegetables Grow Underground

Many vegetables grow
the way carrots do.
Radishes, beets, and parsnips
are other root vegetables.

onions

potatoes

Onions and potatoes start their life in the ground too. Vegetables grown underground give us healthy food to eat.

Glossary

root—an underground plant part that takes in nutrients and water to be used by the plant to grow; some plants grow roots that store a lot of nutrients; people eat these roots as vegetables

seedling—a young plant that has grown from a seed

soil—earth in which plants grow

sprout—to start to grow

stem—the long main part of a plant from which leaves and flowers grow

Read More

Edwards, Nicola. *Vegetables.* See How Plants Grow. New York: PowerKids Press, 2008.

Spilsbury, Louise. *Vegetables.* Eat Smart. Chicago: Heinemann Library, 2009.

Tagliaferro, Linda. *The Life Cycle of a Carrot.* Plant Life Cycles. Mankato, Minn.: Capstone Press, 2007.

Internet Sites

FactHound offers a safe, fun way to find Internet sites related to this book. All of the sites on FactHound have been researched by our staff.

Here's all you do:

Visit *www.facthound.com*

Type in this code: 9781429652803

Check out projects, games and lots more at
www.capstonekids.com

Index

Word Count: 152
Grade: 1
Early-Intervention Level: 21

Editorial Credits
Erika L. Shores, editor; Bobbie Nuytten, designer; Wanda Winch, media researcher;
Laura Manthe, production specialist

Photo Credits
Bill McCarthy, 6 (bottom), 16; Capstone Press: Karon Dubke, 4, 6 (middle, top), 8
(all), 12, 14, 18 (middle), 20 (top); Getty Images: Johanna Parkin, 10; Shutterstock:
Alexey Bragin, cover (soil), Christopher Elwell, 20 (bottom), chungking, (carrot
design element), Irina Zolina, 18 (top), Jo Mikus, 18 (bottom), ultimathule, cover
(carrots)

The author dedicates this book to her friend Gene Mayer, who refuses to eat
vegetables such as carrots and desperately wants to believe beef is a vegetable.